THE CONFESSION OF A LAZY OVERACHIEVER

by LINKED IN AND TOWN HALL ACHIEVER OF THE YEAR
EY NOMINEE ENTREPRENEUR OF THE YEAR
GRAND HOMAGE LYS DIVERSITY
WORLD TOP100 DOCTORS

Dr BAK NGUYEN, DMD

TO ALL THE MILLENNIALS LOOKING TO MAKE THE MOST
OF THEIR TIME ON CAMPUS, BEING LAZY

by Dr BAK NGUYEN

Copyright © 2021 Dr BAK NGUYEN

All rights reserved.

ISBN: 978-1-989536-70-4

Published by: Dr. BAK PUBLISHING COMPANY
Dr.BAK 0089

DISCLAIMER

« The general information, opinions and advice contained in this medium and/or the books, audiobooks, podcasts and publications on Dr. Bak Nguyen's (legal name Dr. Ba Khoa Nguyen) website or social media (hereinafter the "Opinions") present general information on various topics. The Opinions are intended for informational purposes only.

No information contained in the Opinions is a substitute for an expert, consultation, advice or diagnosis. No information contained in the Opinions is a substitute for professional advice and should not be construed as consultation or advice.

Nothing in the Opinions should be construed as professional advice related to the practice of dentistry, medical advice or any other form of legal or financial advice, professional opinion, care or diagnosis, but strictly as general information. All information from the Opinions is for informational purposes only.

Any user who disagrees with the terms of this Disclaimer should immediately cease using or referring to the Opinions. Any action by the user in connection with the information contained in the Opinions is solely at the user's discretion.

The general information contained in the Opinions is provided "as is" and without warranty of any kind, either expressed or implied. Dr. Bak Nguyen (legal name Dr. Ba Khoa Nguyen) makes every effort to ensure that the information is complete and accurate. However, there is no guarantee that the general information contained in the Opinions is always available, truthful, complete, up-to-date or relevant.

The Opinions expressed by Dr. Bak Nguyen (legal name Dr. Ba Khoa Nguyen) are personal and expressed in his own name and do not reflect the opinions of his companies, partners and other affiliates.

Dr. Bak Nguyen (legal name Dr. Ba Khoa Nguyen) also disclaims any responsibility for the content of any hyperlinks included in the Opinions.

Always seek the advice of your expert advisors, physicians or other qualified professionals with any questions you may have regarding your condition. Never disregard professional advice or delay in seeking it because of something you have read, seen or heard in the Opinions. »

ABOUT THE AUTHOR

From Canada, **Dr. BAK NGUYEN**, Nominee Ernst and Young Entrepreneur of the year, Grand Homage Lys DIVERSITY, LinkedIn & TownHall Achiever of the year and TOP 100 Doctors 2021. Dr Bak is a cosmetic dentist, CEO and founder of Mdex & Co. His company is revolutionizing the dental field. Speaker and motivator, he wrote 72 books over 36 months accumulating many world records (to be officialized). His books are covering:

- **ENTREPRENEURSHIP**
- **LEADERSHIP**
- **QUEST OF IDENTITY**
- **DENTISTRY AND MEDICINE**
- **PARENTING**
- **CHILDREN'S BOOKS**
- **PHILOSOPHY**

In 2003, he founded Mdex, a dental company upon which in 2018, he launched the most ambitious private endeavour to reform the dental industry, Canada wide. Philosopher, he has close to his heart the quest of happiness of the people surrounding him, patients and colleagues alike. In 2020, he launched an International collaborative initiative named **THE ALPHAS** to share knowledge and for Entrepreneurs and Doctors to thrive through the Greatest Pandemic and Economic depression of our time.

In 2016, he co-found with Tranie Vo, Emotive World Incorporated, a tech research company to use technology to empower happiness and sharing. U.A.X. the ultimate audio experience is the landmark project on which the team is advancing, utilizing the technics of the movie industry and the advancement in ARTIFICIAL INTELLIGENCE to save the book industry and to upgrade the continuing education space.

These projects have allowed Dr Nguyen to attract interests from the international and diplomatic community and he is now the center of a global discussion in the wellbeing and the future of the health profession. It is in that matter that he shares his thoughts and encourages the health community to share their own stories.

> "It's not worth it go through it alone! Together, we stand, alone, we fall."

Motivational speaker and serial entrepreneur, philosopher and author, from his own words, Dr Nguyen describes himself as a dentist by circumstances, an entrepreneur by nature and a communicator by passion.

He also holds recognitions from the Canadian Parliament and the Canadian Senate.

THE CONFESSION OF A LAZY OVERACHIEVER

by Dr BAK NGUYEN

INTRODUCTION
BY Dr BAK NGUYEN

CHAPTER 1
HOW DO YOU DEFINE LAZINESS?
Dr. BAK NGUYEN

CHAPTER 2
HOW DO YOU DEFINE OVERACHIEVING?
Dr. BAK NGUYEN

CHAPTER 3
WHAT SHOULD I DO IF I HAVE NO MOTIVATION?
Dr. BAK NGUYEN

CHAPTER 4
HOW SHOULD I USE MY TIME MORE WISELY?
Dr. BAK NGUYEN

CHAPTER 5
IS BEING SELF-ABSORB BAD?
Dr. BAK NGUYEN

CHAPTER 6
HOW YOU IMPRESS YOUR CRUSH WITH YOUR LAZINESS?
Dr. BAK NGUYEN

CHAPTER 7
HOW TO EMPOWER YOU TO TRUST YOUR GUT?
Dr. BAK NGUYEN

CHAPTER 8
BEING MOODY, IS IT GOOD OR BAD?
Dr. BAK NGUYEN

CONCLUSION
BY Dr BAK NGUYEN

FOREWORD
"YOUNG, DUMB AND BROKE."
BY JAMIE HUYNH

Young, dumb and broke is my theme song. I am that tropical girl in tank top flipflop, lining up to buy bubble tea every weekend only because I can't afford it every day.

I'm at that point where I borrow my friend's Netflix account but somehow managed to have my own Spotify account. I can be anyone of you who is somewhere in-between trying to live life and trying to escape from it.

I met Dr. Bak on an evening when he was filming for his year-recap project, that was in his Mdex Mansion by the lake. The recap was about such an eventful year within the ALPHAS with lots and lots of achievements.

Like any new employees would do, I come to shake his hands. "Hi, thank you for the opportunity to be a part of your team." I shook his hands thinking now that I have a job, maybe someday I can have a Netflix account of my own without having to share it with anyone.

So, what does a millionaire have anything to do with my world?

When I search for the keyword "lazy quote" on Google, I found 133,000,000 results in 0.46 seconds, and all of that seems to tell you one single thing: *Stop Being Lazy*.

But when I met Dr. Bak, he told me to start being lazy. That stroke me at the deepest of my core! Was that a joke? He was smiling, but not laughing. He was serious!

At that very moment I found out that I share a common thread with successful people. Deep down inside, we are all lazy. Some just try to hide it, some put it out loud. Isn't it funny how we all went through the same journey with emotions, fear, pain, limitation, confusion, and crisis… and come out so differently?

So I ask him, why is that? And here comes a series of questions that all of us will ask ourselves at some point in our life.

Before you keep on reading, this is not like any life-changing book that makes you rich or teaches you how to become a billionaire. Just a book that puts your laziness into good use.

Enjoy.

Jamie

INTRODUCTION
by Dr. BAK NGUYEN

This is a first of many, many things. This is my 89th book, while I have 5 books open to complete. Amongst those 5, 2 are just about editing the chapters of my guest authors, 3 I still have to write. To start yet a new book endeavour seems a little overwhelming at this stage, even for me!

So why am I doing it, you may ask? Well, being a tornado and scoring world record after world record writing books at an accelerating pace, I learnt a long time ago to follow my instincts and to listen to my emotions. My guts and emotions are pushing me to open up, once again, to this new opportunity, to embrace the new.

Last week, I welcomed a new recruit to Dr. Bak's marketing team, Jamie. Jamie is Tranie's cousin. She graduated with a marketing degree and is looking to prove herself. As usual, I stayed open and kind. Open and kind, that doesn't mean to give her the wheel. We had a few exchanges.

Jamie is young and hopeful. She does not have the ambition to change the world but to find her place in the world. She can work hard (that, she has proven moving to Canada by herself a few years ago, looking for a better future) but she will be very selective about her battles. Like most the millennials of her generation, Jamie is looking for happiness and freedom… and she is expecting to find success on the way.

To me, that sounded very challenging but I took the time to hear her out. I did not try to stop nor to convert her, I simply listen and put myself in her shoes, in the shoes of a whole generation. Lately, COVID did reboot everything, why not take the opportunity to learn from our next generation?

I must confess, not all of Jamie's concerns were of the same importance. To her, being a millionaire is so far away in her list of priorities and from her own words, may not even be a possibility. On the other hand, to overachieve, that was something well within reach. And this is how she perceived me, as a millionaire overachiever.

The overachiever was appealing to her, not the millionaire. I have to say how surprised I was. Not by the rhetoric but by the perception. I am not a millionaire and an overachiever, I am first and foremost a stubborn lazy guy. That being said, I do because I feel and I am successful because I do not give up until I am satisfied. Somehow, that came to be known as overachieving.

And what do I do when I scored big? Well, I celebrate for an evening and as the feeling fades away, I am dedicated to find it again, walking another journey. To me, this has nothing to do with overachieving anything, it is about keeping the fun and the run.

Doing so for the last decade, I became a millionaire from my decisions and actions. The irony is that I became a millionaire from the decisions and actions that required less and less of my time and energy.

You see, I am a doctor in dentistry because of my parents. Being the son of immigrants, I was raised to please my parents. And pleasing them meant to be good at school until you have the 2 letters of D and R in front of your name. That was no easy task. Not easy to be admitted, not easy to graduate and even harder to perform every day, day after day. It takes dedication, discipline, and passion.

Despite my preferences for arts and communication, I gave in to pleasing my parents. Back in dental school, I was so bored that I started an independent movie production. That brought me to the doors of Hollywood and to the blink of my self-destruction. But then, I was too exhausted and tired to keep betting against the odds. Once more, I gave in to what my parents and Society wanted out of me. I became a dentist.

It took me a year to learn to become a good dentist, and then, a great one. I became a great dentist not because I was the best but because I was loved by my patients. And I was loved because I cared.

You see, most of my patients do not like dentists. They do not want to be there. Guess what? Me neither! On that, we connected. After that, it was a matter of getting the necessary out of the way and to keep connecting. 20 years within the profession and I became known for my humanity, my emotional intelligence.

"I TREAT PEOPLE, NOT TEETH."
Dr. BAK NGUYEN

I built a company that has a shot to change the entire dental industry and how my profession is perceived by the general public. I wrote books and gave conferences and interviews on my views to humanize dental medicine. I am loved and much appreciated by my patients. I spend half of my vital energy and time dedicated to my patients, my profession. I still do not like dental surgery but my patients, I love.

That kept the lights up and gave me a great living. But that did not make me into a millionaire. That might surprised you, it shocked me the first time I realized that too. But then, it started to make sense. You'll see it too, as we are moving forward in our journey together.

So I achieved and overachieved at my tasks. That brought me success and recognition. Lately, I have been received as one of the world's **TOP100 doctors**. It is a huge honour and such a surprise… for someone who never wanted to be a doctor in the first place. **Overachieving** got me there.

What got me to become a **millionaire** is a whole other story. Yes, it requires discipline, learning, and resilience but it asked for so much less compared to medicine and surgery! The first time I reached the status of millionaire, I was doing something I swore never to do: invest in real estate.

Younger, my parents had income properties. We, my siblings and I, served as workforce. Weekends and summer vacations were often spent going back and forth to those income properties. We were all mad about it. Then, my mother told us what she thought was the absolute truth: "Study and work hard to become doctors and you will never have to do this again."

That worked like a charm. My 2 siblings and myself, we all became doctors and dentists to never have to work on income properties ever again. But if I recall correctly, this was about working hard? 7 years into the profession, I realized that I was working harder and harder and that I was nowhere close to accumulating any wealth nor reserve for the rainy days. I was very successful, I had a huge credit score, but I was always on the line. If I fail or fall sick, that could jeopardize everything.

I read all the books on personal finance, motivation, and personal growth that I could find. And then, I remembered that I forgot my true nature: I am a lazy guy working much too hard! I then leveraged on my own nature to make my next moves.

Fast forward 12 years later, I am a millionaire, overachiever, industries disruptor, CEO, world record author, TOP100 doctor… and a world-class lazy guy! How about that for a confession?!

Within this journey, **THE CONFESSION OF A LAZY OVERACHIEVER**, you will be sharing my conversation with Jamie as I am, not trying to convince her of my ways of thinking but as I am putting myself in her shoes and see how I would be playing it, if I was a millennial on campus, knowing what I know today.

I started this chapter by saying that this was a first of many things. Well, **CONFESSION** is just not part of my lexicon, and yet, somehow, it is the bold title of my next book. I never hid the fact that I was lazy but to create a new franchise of books and podcast title **LAZY**, this is bold, even for me.

I was so genuine and true about my openness that I even accepted a completely new design of my books' covers, changing the Dr. Bak's brand! This shocked all of my team. Looking at the cover of this book, you don't know how insecure I am… and I am many things but insecure is not one of them.

"CONFIDENCE IS SEXY."
Dr. BAK NGUYEN

Maybe that is what it is, to confess. Maybe this is what it feels like to open up and to strip down of our shields, armours, and titles. But you know what? It felt right, it felt good because it is genuine. Writing this book, I felt young and hopeful just like back in my days on campus.

This is **THE CONFESSION OF A LAZY OVERACHIEVER**. Welcome to the Alphas.

> THE WORD LAZY IS WHAT PEOPLE IN CONTROL
> LIKE TO LABEL OUR YOUTH WITH,
> NOT JUST ON WHAT TO DO BUT ALSO ON HOW TO DO IT.
> PLAY IT SMART TO ACHIEVE AND CHILL.
>
> Dr. BAK NGUYEN

CHAPTER 1
HOW DO YOU DEFINE LAZINESS?

"BEING LAZY DOESN'T MEAN THAT YOU DON'T HAVE TO DO SHIT, IT MEANS THAT YOU DON'T HAVE TO GO THROUGH SHIT TO GET THINGS DONE."

BY DR. BAK NGUYEN

We are not wasting any time here, I love that! What does that mean to be lazy? Well, let's clear out the air, being lazy is not just laying around all day long doing nothing. Being lazy, if you want to leverage it, means to not waste your time on trivial stuff.

> "BEING LAZY DOESN'T MEAN THAT YOU DON'T HAVE TO DO SHIT, IT MEANS THAT YOU DON'T HAVE TO GO THROUGH SHIT TO GET THINGS DONE."
> Dr. BAK NGUYEN

I have no better way to say it, excuse my vocabulary. But that is exactly how I rose from the noise, the expectations, the requirements, the frustration, and the pain. I can work and put in the effort, as soon as I can see the worth. All of you will agree with that.

Well, lazy is what people in control use to qualify us every time they want us to do something that we do not want to do or that we do not understand. To them, blind obedience is good, everything else is evil or lazy. Do I have to say more?

Very young, we have been trained to think that laziness is a bad thing. Then, to please the authorities, we conformed and went along, pushing through the stages and the boundaries, often without asking questions. Scratch that. We did ask questions, and often, the answer that we received made no sense, coming with an attitude to discourage the next question we might have… And we learnt to comply.

"PERFECTION IS A LIE."
Dr. BAK NGUYEN

I will never repeat that one enough, perfection is a lie. Even if it makes much sense, it is made after the fact and customized to fit the narrative. **Nothing is ever perfect.** We make the most with what we have and with the time in hand, that's it.

Some times it turns out ok, some other times, it turns out great, and, unfortunately, some other times, it will be a mess. For as long as we gave it our best without holding back, there was nothing more we could do.

And what if it happens again? Well, we will do the most with what we have, within the time that we will dispose. That being said, we will have more experience, so things should be easier, right? Well, know that no two situations are exactly the same, so no solution can be copied and pasted that simply. So even with more experience, it is not necessarily easier.

Even worse, with the false belief that with experience, we now know how, we might be blinded to the current situation and to address it the wrong way, just because we had a recipe in hand… perhaps, it was the wrong recipe…

Forget about perfection and to find the perfect recipe to life. That's is my wisest advice to all of you. And yet, we should leverage upon the past to deal with the future, so how do it? Before I answer that question, I would like to bring your attention to **LEVERAGING**.

> "IF YOU ARE LOOKING TO BE LAZY, LEARN TO LEVERAGE!"
> Dr. BAK NGUYEN

And what is leveraging? Well, it is to look at the past models and templates that could help us deal with the present and the future. Nothing is completely new, just like nothing is completely the same. Not just events but people too. Just like they say, History repeats itself, so are people too.

People are driven by emotions and desires. People are trained with culture and folklore, we called that education. Well, in modern words, this is how they got programmed. Education is the program, predicting the behaviours while the emotions and desires are the triggers. No one can know in advance how one will react in the absolute, but considering his or her program (education and culture), we can predict with much accuracy his or her reaction.

So contrary to the general belief, it is not the event that we can understand, those are usually out of our hands (unless you are the one responsible for the change itself). To the events, we react, after the facts. But most of the time, we are not just reacting to the events but to the people, and people we can study and predict their reactions.

People react based on who they are and what they are feeling. This is on an individual basis. Gathered in a crowd, the reaction of people is event more predictable, most will be following the crowd, moving as a herd. Study the herd and you can map the future! Study people and you can predict the future.

Don't waste your time trying to control the events. But just like people, you can study the event to understand how they come to be and then, look for the signs. And yes, they are always signs.

So being lazy, I studied people, events, and crowds? I studied the systems. Biology, economy, politics, education, those are all systems. I started this chapter by telling you that being lazy is not to hand around doing nothing, so yes, you will have to study. I also told you that being lazy also means not having to go through shit to get things done.

Forget perfection and the recipes. Study the templates, study History, and study psychology. Myths and legends are templates of our folklore and behaviours. History is a great portrait of the past that, too often, serves as a template to repaint the future. And psychology, well, if everything changes, human psychology is amongst the steadiest things that stood the challenge of centuries and millennials.

You want to be lazy, to spend as least time as possible studying? Well, study what you are dealing with every day, people! You want to study people and still, you are too lazy to open a book? Look in the mirror and try to understand the person looking back at you. That's half of all the equation you will face every day already. Understand yourself and then, you'll see, it will be easier to understand people and the events…

So what does it mean to be lazy? Well, it is to cut through the crap and the filters, and to go straight to the point. Does that mean that we must forget about civilities and politeness? Absolutely not, it is not because you understood the situation, that you are good to go. You still need to interact with the other party to fix whatever situation you are in. So stay polite and build that *bridge*!

In other words, I study people and events (science) to have templates to speed up my reaction when facing challenges. I know that they are templates, nothing more, but applying those templates to people and events, I now have a frame of reference to understand quickly what is true and what is not. Even if my template was 100% wrong, seeing that, now points me in the right direction!

> **"I STUDY TO BE LAZY. I CHOOSE WHAT I STUDY TO BE SMARTER."**
> Dr. BAK NGUYEN

On that, here is a great piece of advice: don't study everything, it is not true that studying is always good. Studying is programming your brain and body to react, so you must study what will be of use to you. Of course, most of our lives, other people chose for us, chose what is good for us and we did not have the luxury of choosing what we are studying. You cannot be more wrong!

If you stop at the first step, what is forced on you, you may be right. Have you ever heard that education will buy you a job and self-education will build you a living? I hope that I came up with that one but I did not. I did benefit greatly from its wisdom though.

Do what is asked of you because it is simpler and required less work than to rebel. It is also the best way to fight procrastination. Do what is asked of you. Then, as you react to that, use these emotions of yours to study whatever you deem right!

A simple example, back at school, I hated science. I was good at it but it did not fire any passion in me. Instead, I was attracted to history, myths, and legends. Well, to escape death by boredom, I read most of the Greek mythology and the biography of most of the great figures of occidental History.

I self-educated myself, leveraging on my emotions and the time I was condemned in school. If I was free and at home, I am not sure that I would have read and discovered as much.

By being lazy, I obeyed because it was the shortest way out. But school is not about assignments, one can't leave as he or she is done. Being benched at school is about time! So I made the most of that time, escaping to Universes of my choosing while trying to get out of those forced on me.

Well, I developed speed and ease in the mandatory subjects. Then, reading about the myths and legends, I discovered that many if not all of the traits could be found looking at my teachers and fellow students. I understood jealousy and rivalry. I understood mind games and kindness, I understood generosity and politics. I was not looking to control but now I know when I am being controlled or manipulated. The signs are now obvious to me.

As they were busy looking down on their assignments, procrastinating, or thinking of rebellion, I was looking at them and learnt to read the signs. This is how I came to study every day, day after day. I studied because I am lazy, I obeyed. Then, I studied because I discovered the templates and an easier way to map my surroundings.

Today, I am looked up to help and to guide people. I wrote a library of books mainly based on human behaviours and how to leverage it. Finance, communication, medicine, politics, education, philosophy, love, everything is based and tainted with human emotions and psychology.

> "BEING LAZY DOESN'T MEAN THAT YOU DON'T HAVE TO DO SHIT, IT MEANS THAT YOU DON'T HAVE TO GO THROUGH SHIT TO GET THINGS DONE."
> Dr. BAK NGUYEN

This is **THE CONFESSION OF A LAZY OVERACHIEVER**. Welcome to the Alphas.

> THE WORD LAZY IS WHAT PEOPLE IN CONTROL LIKE TO LABEL OUR YOUTH WITH, NOT JUST ON WHAT TO DO BUT ALSO ON HOW TO DO IT. PLAY IT SMART TO ACHIEVE AND CHILL.
>
> Dr. BAK NGUYEN

CHAPTER 2
HOW DO YOU DEFINE OVERACHIEVING?

"YOU CANNOT AIM TO OVERACHIEVE TRYING TO OVERACHIEVE. IT'S ALL ABOUT GROWING."
BY DR. BAK NGUYEN

I started this discussion by saying how surprised I was with Jamie more interested in my **OVERACHIEVER** status than my **MILLIONAIRE** status. To her, to overachieve is much more within reach than to become a millionaire.

To be frank, I will say that it is the opposite. When you have studied the systems and understood the game, being a millionaire isn't that hard. What is hard is to work to earn that million! No surprise here!

Think with me for a minute, if you work to earn a million in cash, how long do you have to work to earn as much? You will need to work to earn 2 million since the government will be taking half!

So 2 million, even at an hourly rate of $200 an hour (which is tremendous by the way) will require you to work 10 000 hours. Considering that you are working 8 hours a day, this is 1250 working days. In other words, 3.42 years, working 7 days a week.

Not bad will you say. Can you earn $200 an hour and do that for 3 years and a half while not spending a single penny? To me, this is wishful thinking… To most, $20 an hour is much closer to reality… so 34.2 years not spending a penny and working 8 hours a day. You see the point.

Overachieving here will mean that you will try to overwork and to outsmart everyone else to increase your return from

$20 an hour to $200 and then, to $2000. The chances that this happen and that you are surviving the process are slim to none but it is possible.

You can also work more hours, instead of 8 hours a day, you can go for 10 or even 12. How long do you think you can last doing so?

> "YOU CAN'T BE A SQUIRREL AND HOPE TO EAT THE LION'S SHARE."
> Dr. BAK NGUYEN

The worse part is that as you start succeeding to accumulate something worth talking about, a slightly bigger bully will try to take it away from you. This is a classic, this is life.

So then, how come so many people have reached this kind of wealth and so much more? Because they studied a system and have learnt to leverage that system.

The question was how do I define overachieving. I gave you a great example to understand that I do not define nor care about overachieving. I care about results. And since, like you, I have a short attention span, the faster the better!

Overachieving is not something I was aiming for nor had in my lexicon. But over time, this is how people describe me. The first person to do so and who's words touched my heart was my oldest friend, my best friend from high school. A respected surgeon himself, he never shied away from the challenges to achieve the goals he has in mind. Thanks to his words, I understood how people saw me for the first time: as an overachiever.

Let's define what he was describing. I wasn't nearly as successful as I am today. I haven't started changing the world nor writing any single book yet but I was someone with dreams and the determination to see them through.

By that time, I had more failures than successes. But that was me looking at my belly button. In comparison with the other people, I was delivering and overdelivering while they were talking and thinking. That's the definition of an overachiever from my oldest friend, Dr. Hugo Diec.

So yes, on that, Jamie was right, overachieving may be more accessible than becoming a millionaire. So then, how does one overachieve? Trust me on that, one has to be very stubborn to overachieve anything in our society. We are all about balance and average, and standards. No overachiever can ever come out under these conditions. It is simply too hard.

> "THE MINUTE THAT YOU DO A LITTLE MORE, THE AVERAGE WILL BE PULLING YOU DOWN."
> Dr. BAK NGUYEN

To overdo something is never good, ever. Keep that in mind. This is true from the perspective in the present tense. To look back on something, anything, we do not look at the process but rather the result. If the results are great, only then, we will be interested to analyze the process in order to reproduce it.

Well, when you are labelling someone as an overachiever, you do not look at his or her process but at his or her results. Say what you may but this is a hard fundamental truth.

So back at my surprise between overachiever and millionaire, to me, a millionaire is the result, tangible and verifiable. How that person made it? Overachieving might be an ingredient, an important one but just one ingredient.

I am lazy, remember? If overachieving is overworking, don't count on me. To have an idea and to see it through, that has always been who I am. Well, take that trait of character and fast forward it in time and you will find an overachiever.

In other words, I have been an overachiever most of my life. Was I worth your time and attention as much? No, because I had no result to show for. I was a hard worker and a dreamer but one that still needed to find his Destiny first.

And I met with my Destiny the day I made peace with myself. I made peace with the doctor that Society and my parent forged out of me, I made peace with the artist and sensitive soul I trapped in a box for close to 2 decades. I made peace that I am of 2 different natures trapped into one soul.

The day that I accepted my role as a doctor in Society, I found success, average success. The day that I forgave myself to have locked away my artistic side and creativity, I found peace and reunification. That day, I feel at ease and at peace, knowing who I was. No words, no labels, no expectations could get to me anymore.

Suddenly, it was not about success or failure anymore but about living my life and making the most of it. I started to be aware of my instincts and feelings. I was 35 the day I finally made peace with myself. That was 9 years ago.

From there, my decisions and actions changed by a few degrees. I wasn't looking to please anymore, I was looking for results. I remained a dentist and keep taking care of my patients, I got better and better at my mission. That growth exploded exponentially as I decided to take care of not only my patients but of my peers too. **Mdex & Co** came on the table to revolutionize the dental industry.

Then, to be consequential with my actions, I needed to embrace the stage to convince people of my views and different perspectives. I took the stage but instead of convincing people with my ideas, I shared my experience as an entrepreneur, a CEO, a doctor, and, as my books were piling up, as a human being.

Today I address you as a man walking his journey, nothing more. Somehow along the way, the **OVERACHIEVER** status got lost. It is still present in my titles and announcements but very rarely it will make it passed the introduction.

So how do I define overachieving? I simply don't. It is not important. What is important to my eyes is to find out you each of us is, deep down, to make peace with that and to let it be. To let us be.

How do I come to have others see me as an overachiever? Well, the short answer is to deliver results, not just consistently but to build upon your last win to deliver the next one, *a little bigger, a little faster, a little crazier*. By doing so, you will have fun discovering your potentials and powers.

Oh, and one last thing on the matter. You can discover your power as much as you want but **never forget your environment**. If you are rising and people around are not, you just made yourself many, many enemies. Use your power to serve others, not just those you know but be open to serve and to empower those who are coming to you. Helping them is your best way to overachieve, to overdeliver, and to grow exponentially.

You overachieve because since it is for the good of someone else, it is never too much. You overdeliver because since you are looking to please, the happier there are, the better you feel. And you are growing exponentially since you are evolving without resistance. It is always harder when you are the center of the discussion, your own emotions are often stacked against you.

> "TAKING CARE OF SOMEONE ELSE, YOU DO NOT HAVE TO DEAL WITH YOUR OWN EMOTIONS, ELIMINATING MOST OF THE RESISTANCE TO YOUR GROWTH."
> Dr. BAK NGUYEN

So don't waste your time looking to overachieve or to figure out what it means. Find yourself and listen to that inner voice. As you feel what you need to do, do not stop until you have concrete results.

Build on your previous win and do it again, a little bigger, a little better, a little faster. And if you want a cheat, use your powers to serve others, there is much less resistance on the way.

I am lazy, where ever there is less resistance, I am in!

This is **THE CONFESSION OF A LAZY OVERACHIEVER**. Welcome to the Alphas.

THE WORD LAZY IS WHAT PEOPLE IN CONTROL
LIKE TO LABEL OUR YOUTH WITH,
NOT JUST ON WHAT TO DO BUT ALSO ON HOW TO DO IT.
PLAY IT SMART TO ACHIEVE AND CHILL.

Dr. BAK NGUYEN

CHAPTER 3
WHAT SHOULD I DO IF I HAVE NO MOTIVATION?

"THAT'S OFTEN AN ENVIRONMENTAL PROBLEM."
BY DR. BAK NGUYEN

Well, motivation is such a broad concept. Unless it is a primary need as to feet, to find shelter, to reproduce, and to belong, it is not simple to self-motivate.

On that, we need to study the pyramid of Abraham Maslow, one of the great figures of modern psychology. Trust me, this is one of the fastest ways to understand motivation and human behaviour.

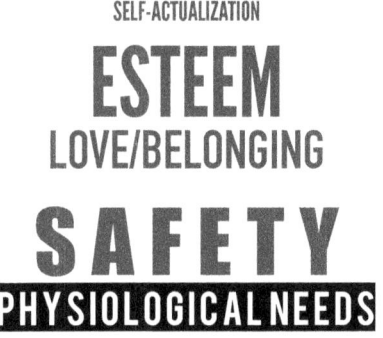

THE PYRAMID OF ABRAHAM MASLOW

Motivation is nothing but a trigger to push us into action. As we go hungry, we will be looking to eat. To hunt, to fish, to trade, everything one needs to do to eat. As the hunger for food is satisfied, we are moving up the ladder of needs, moving to safety, in other words, the need to find shelter. Once more, we will do what it takes to satisfy that need.

Once our primary needs satisfied, we will move forward to the need to belong and the need for love. In both situations, it is about regrouping with other individuals. If social aptitudes were helpful until here, the middle of the pyramid of Maslow is all about social behaviours: how we are welcomed and perceived by others and how we react to them.

Then, after that, we belong to a group and feel secure about that, from love, friendship, or any other kind of relationship (religion, status, preferences, ...) we will eventually feel the need for more. We will now need to feel appreciated and respected for who we are.

Until now, we were very satisfied to belong to a group, to be amongst the average of that group. Suddenly, we will feel the need to be unique. This will mess up everything we fought so hard to achieve until that point. To be unique is to be above or below the average, it is to be alone and isolated. If that wasn't enough, to look for self-esteem will also mean to compare ourselves with others to know who is on top of who.

This is not a behaviour unique to Humans but also to most animals living in herds. First, it's about connecting and then, it's about differentiation, to know who is on top. In our vocabulary, it is about connecting or comparing.

Well, basic psychology will tell you that the energy will increase as you are connecting and will decrease as you are comparing. That being said, there is no way for an individual to break from the group without disconnecting… and those are the ones moving in a solo path. For others, the path to uniqueness is to compare and fight until they are the last one standing on top. Once again, the energy is going down.

This is why it is so hard to move from love and belonging to esteem since no matter the path chosen, the energy will be decreasing drastically before it could go up. But once esteem reach, to move to the top of the Pyramid of needs is a straight path.

So this chapter was about motivation. What about motivation. If we understood the breakdown of the Pyramid of Needs, we know that our body will be motivated to satisfy hungers. From hungers to sheltering, it is a straight line. Arriving to love and belonging is a straight line, gathering more and more energy. And from there, the motivation got lost, since we will have to accept a decrease of energy first before continuing our ascension.

Add to that the evolution in our society. Hunger for food and for shelter is something that more and more individuals consider as entitlements. And this is a great thing. With the decrease of religion in our folklore and since the advent of contraception, the hunger for sex is also considered more and more mundane.

We are breaded into life and most of the time, we inherit the social status of our parents, so belonging is also part of our social starting package… this and the love from our parents and family.

This is a great social progress of our civilization, to start right at the middle of the Pyramid of Maslow. But it also has its side effects. Moving forward, who of you is willing to lose first (energy) before rising? This is individual ambition and aspiration. What about the overprotective parents that are looking to protect their kids from all the dangers of the world? This is another string keeping you inside your comfort zone.

And let say that you are ambitious and curious enough to break free from what you know and that your parents encourage you to fly with your own wings, it does not get any easier, even with these two are coming together. Your siblings and friends, those you were averaging with, as they are not ready to leave the nest and to break from their comfort zone, how do you think that they will react?

They will do everything in their power to keep you from leaving. Love, loyalty, friendship will be the first words they will use. Then, it will be about duty and being realistic. If that does not work, they will start to curse you and some will even try to shoot you down in the back as you are trying your wings for the first time.

Do not worry, it was not about you. It was about them. Nothing they do can affect you unless you let them. That being said, even once you've left and started to gain some altitude after the initial fall, they will be spreading bad things about you. Why? Because you are reminding them of the hard decisions that they haven't dare to answer for themselves yet. That's why they hated you so much, you the brother, you the sister, and now, the traitor!

Is this ring a bell in any of you? This is a classic of human behaviour, only, somehow, our leaders and teachers, never thought that it was important enough to include in our *mandatory time on the bench*!

So back to motivation, what about motivation? Some of you are ambitious and curious by nature. You will be amongst the first ones to leave the nest and to jump, no matter what people think of you. You are the lucky one, to you, it was simpler. Not just simpler but also easier since you jumped at the first opening that you saw.

> "THE LONGER ONE STAY AT THE EDGE OF THE CLIFF LOOKING DOWN, THE HARDER IT WILL BE TO JUMP."
> Dr. BAK NGUYEN

Then, they are those amongst you which your parents and teachers pushed forward to jump. You hated that but you too did not grow roots at the edge of the cliff. (Cutting those roots will not be an easy task). To have empowering parents and teachers are surely amongst the precious gifts in this world.

Then, there is the rest of you who will have to face the cliff and jump by your own will before Life pushes you into the abyss. It will be hard and very painful because there is the fear and the pain of the amputation of the roots you grew standing on the edge for so long… add to that the atrophy of the wings you've never exercised.

So where are you standing in the process and the pyramid of Maslow? You know that sooner or later, you will have to jump. We are born how we are, the only thing one can do is to be aware of that and make peace with it. We do not choose our parents, so it is irrelevant to blame them.

And it is our turn to stand on the cliff and to spread our wings, well, the only thing that we can do is to know that what we are feeling is normal and most people are going through the same doubts and fears. We each have our unique story, but this was part of evolution.

Evolution is about change. For most, it is hard to change unless the pain was greater than the fear of change. And this is when Life will be pushing you down the *abyss*, looking to see if you can make use of your wings… those you may never even knew that you had.

> **"MOST OF THE TIME, THE PAIN HAS TO BE BIGGER THAN THE PAIN OF CHANGE, FOR CHANGE TO HAPPEN."**
> Dr. BAK NGUYEN

So to you on campus, what does that mean? Don't slap yourself in the face as you are looking for motivation. You were very, very comfortable in the middle of the pyramid and within the average.

To break from that, even if it is natural, will feel not natural to you at first (decrease in energy). That's normal and everybody is going through the same process. Find comfort in that.

Once again, I can't explain why most teaching institutions never find it important enough to have included in your mandatory time, just like they never deem important to teach us about personal finance nor taxes. And yet, those are the standards in our modern society.

Motivation comes from needs. Motivation comes from desires. Motivation comes with ambition. Motivation comes with curiosity. Rarely motivation will come from fear, manipulation does!

So listen to your needs and get motivated. Take the time to understand your inner-self and motivation will rise by itself. Very rarely, motivation will be found looking around, especially from the people in your surrounding.

This is **THE CONFESSION OF A LAZY OVERACHIEVER**. Welcome to the Alphas.

> THE WORD LAZY IS WHAT PEOPLE IN CONTROL
> LIKE TO LABEL OUR YOUTH WITH,
> NOT JUST ON WHAT TO DO BUT ALSO ON HOW TO DO IT.
> PLAY IT SMART TO ACHIEVE AND CHILL.
>
> Dr. BAK NGUYEN

CHAPTER 4
HOW SHOULD I USE MY TIME MORE WISELY?

"LISTEN TO YOUR NEEDS AND LEVERAGE YOUR HORMONES."
BY DR. BAK NGUYEN

This should be an easy one, how do you have better use of your time? Your generation, the millennials have escaped much of the *clipping* and *formatting* that the previous generations went through to fit **Conformity**. The decrease of the influence of religion within our schooling systems should have played a major role in western societies.

In short, as the previous generations were shaped to ignore their needs and to keep in line hoping that their effort and sacrifice will eventually be rewarded, your generation (millennials) have been raised to expect your needs and desires to be **met without or with little sacrifice**.

I am not taking anything away from you, your parents worked pretty hard to make sure that you have everything that you need and want to be happy. They gave you more than they received, following the trend begun by their own parents, your grandparents.

If 2 generations ago, **war and hunger** were part of the daily worries, in many parts of the world, abundance and social evolution make sure to keep wars and hunger at bay. Since the 2nd world war, many organizations and regulations have been put in place *to buffer* the basics needs at the bottom of the Pyramid of Maslow.

We each have our own opinion of how that happened but I think that we owe much gratitude to the women and men who built and led the **United Nations** and their derivatives.

No, the world is not perfect but considering where we were a few decades earlier, we made significant progress.

As a result, the younger generations have been raised in *abundance* and the needs are less and less of a concern since it has become what the oldest generations are calling *entitlement*. This is no judgment, just the establishment of facts and causal effect to understand how it happened.

Since most of your needs are not strong triggers to motivate you anymore (thanks or because of the *Age of Abundance*), you are left only with your desires to trigger your *hormonal response*. And yes, the Pyramid of Maslow was only the mapping of your mind. To that map, your body is responding with its messengers: **HORMONES**.

Everything that you feel is caused by the release of a specific chemical in your body. As you are hungry, your body produces a chemical to make your entire body knows (and feel) the hunger, monopolizing most of your resources until you satisfy that hunger.

Something else you have to understand how your body is built:

> **"THERE IS NO HALFWAY OR BALANCE WITH YOUR HORMONES, IT IS ALL OR NOTHING!"**

This means that you cannot half feel something. We are talking about *sensations* here, not *emotions*. When you are hungry, you are really hungry. When you feel the need to have sex, you really feel the desire fuelling your veins. When you feel under threat, you will feel it with all of your body.

In the stock market, it is well known that all traders are driven by either **GREED** or **FEAR**, there is nothing in between. Those 2 are the *all-or-nothing responses* our body is hardwired to respond to. Even if one will go from one to the next like changing master, one will never serve both *masters* at the same time.

Once again, this is how or chemicals are released and how our bodies work. No one can experience **GREED** and **FEAR** at the same time. They might think they are but that in their heads, they cannot feel both at the same time within their guts, within their bodies.
Is there really nothing between **GREED** and **FEAR**? Actually, there is: confusion and stalling, in other words, **FROZEN** and indecision. Being **FROZEN** is not a hormonal response, but it is a phase between the hormonal response of **GREED** and **FEAR**.

Once **FROZEN**, it will take an even bigger hormonal response from your body to kick you back on your feet to feel **GREED** or **FEAR**. Do you start to understand your own behaviours? I bet you can now see a clear image of your past flashing before your eyes. Now you know. Now you understand.

> **"STUDY THE SYSTEMS, THOSE ARE THE KEY TO LEVERAGE YOUR LAZINESS."**
> Dr. BAK NGUYEN

When I told you to look in the mirror to understand the world surrounding you, that's part of what I meant. Understanding how your body works and you will understand how most bodies work.

> **"NO TWO PEOPLE ARE EXACTLY THE SAME BUT VERY FEW WILL LEAVE THE TRACKS AND THE TEMPLATES."**
> Dr. BAK NGUYEN

The tracks and templates, those are the *cookie cutters* we called *culture, education and folklore*. Put the human body, any human body within a specific situation, its first response will be base our its hormonal response (chemical) following the mapping of the Pyramid of Maslow. To understand and to predict the nuances, then, add the filters of *culture, education, folklore,* and *training* and you have predicted the behaviours of most if not all of your subjects.

The closer you get to the base of the Pyramid of needs, the fewer options that subject will have in his or her response.

Eventually, it will boil down to the basic instincts: flight or fight.

"IN OTHER WORDS TO KILL OR BE KILLED..."

And this is the basis of your body, our system. Deep down, we are animals. Millennials of evolution and training got us to evolve and to be civilized. We built on top of the primitive layer but once faced with life-threatening situations, it will not take long before our primitive instincts take over. This wasn't a question of moral or even one of choice, it was simply our response to the chemical released in our body.

Understanding that, can use that as leverage to self-motivate? To fight procrastination and to avoid the **FROZEN** stage? Absolutely. Keep in mind that the body will release its hormonal response based on triggers, and those triggers are mostly in your minds.

Your parents successfully raised you above the primary needs (hunger, safety, and even kept you safe in love and belonging). What you have at your disposal as triggers are your **Desires**. Use those as triggers. Train your mind to feel your desire at a deeper degree so eventually, it will trick your body to release the same kind of hormones.

HUNGER is **GREED**. And since your body will respond with an *all-or-nothing response*, as soon as your body has associated **GREED** to the primary response of **HUNGER**, you will now have the **POWER OF THE HORMONES** to monopolize all of your resources.

It will take time and dedication but just like the athletes and champions who trained day in and day out to become addicted to the hormone of victory (*endorphin*) which most athletes will say that it tops an orgasm. Now you understand the **POWER OF THE HORMONES**.

To find motivation in your brain, day in and day out, takes much energy. Why not let your body do the work for you? Hack your way into the blueprint of your body and leverage your instincts and their power mechanisms. Use your desires as triggers and do that day after day, eventually, your body will follow… and so will the superpowers coming with its hormonal response.

Please do not misunderstand my words in here. I never told you to use your desires to trigger someone else into satisfying your needs. I told you to use your desires to push yourself into action.

In the previous question, you wanted to know how to motivate yourself, your complete answer is to feel. What you just understood here is that I wasn't talking about feeling your emotions but your hormones.

Don't discard your emotions either, there are your triggers. Train yourself to listen to your emotions (desires) and to really focus on them until its hurts. Don't go to anyone for help, you will need to feel the *hunger of that void*. Doing so, you are training your body to respond to that desire of yours as if it was an exterior stimulus.

Hold the *pain* for long enough and your body will respond with all of its might, releasing the *flight or fight hormonal response*. Then, don't sit down on both your hands wondering what just happened, use that boost in energy and concentration to take the actions you lacked the motivation or courage to take until that point.

This is a simple law of physic. It will take much energy to move a body in *inertia*. Once that body is moving, it will take less energy to keep it in motion. Actually, it will take just enough energy to **overcome** the *resistance*.

Then, if you keep accelerating the movement, the body will reach a pace where its own mass will now contribute to its speed. From that point, it will take more energy to stop the motion than to keep it moving. You just discover the **POWER OF MOMENTUM**.

This is **THE CONFESSION OF A LAZY OVERACHIEVER**. Welcome to the Alphas.

THE WORD LAZY IS WHAT PEOPLE IN CONTROL
LIKE TO LABEL OUR YOUTH WITH,
NOT JUST ON WHAT TO DO BUT ALSO ON HOW TO DO IT.
PLAY IT SMART TO ACHIEVE AND CHILL.

Dr. BAK NGUYEN

CHAPTER 5
IS BEING SELF-ABSORB BAD?

"IF YOU NEVER TALK ABOUT YOURSELF, IT IS THEN ALL ABOUT YOUR DOUBTS AND FEARS... EVEN WHEN YOU WERE NOT CONCERNED!"

BY DR. BAK NGUYEN

What a beautiful question! Of course, it is good to be aware of who you are and to listen to your needs, that's the only way to leverage your own emotions. We covered that within the last 2 questions.

That being said, being self-centred is good since it is how you can become confident and open up to the world without tainting everything with your fears and doubts.

Yes, unfortunately, those who, in the fear of being self-absorbed, lack taking the time to know who they are, even without being aware, will taint everything they touch with their doubts and fears.

> "THE ONLY WAY TO HELP SOMEONE ELSE IS TO BE SECURE FIRST."
> Dr. BAK NGUYEN

And what is being secure mean? It means to be confident enough to let go of who we are to be 100% available to the other. I am talking about helping others, well it goes much broader than that. Only once you are comfortable with who you are, can you really love someone else.

Only once you are secured, can you forget about yourself. Being secure does not mean having all the answers. Being secured means knowing who you are and what you are capable of. This will keep doubts far away. As a surgeon, I learnt very soon within my practice.

"YOU CAN'T POUR MUCH FROM AN EMPTY CUP."

A little in the same vein, when you are in an airplane, you are instructed that in case of emergency, to wear your oxygen mask first before helping those around you. This is not selfishness, it is about logic and efficiency to increase the chances of survival of both parties. Being aware of yourself and your needs is the exact same thing.

That being said, this is about being self-centered, which everyone is. Do you remember the Pyramid of Maslow? Being hungry was about you. Looking for shelter was also about you. Having the urge to reproduce, once more, that was about you again!

Only once you've reached the 3rd level, as you belong in a group, that idea of the others started to take more importance. Anyone saying otherwise is simply hypocrite, ignorant, or simply lying.

"TO BE SELFLESS, YOU MUST FIRST BE SELF-AWARE."
Dr. BAK NGUYEN

So no, being self-aware has nothing to do with being selfish. Now what about being self-absorbed? We are playing with words in here… know who you are first, be comfortable with who you are, and only then, can you deal with other people.

In that answer, the other people were an important part of the equation. If being self-absorbed means not seeing anything else but yourself, well, unfortunately, you have missed the point. You must know yourself first to see, understand, and eventually deal with the other. Without the other, there is much less meaning in understanding yourself, from a social standpoint.

So to have a clear answer, it is okay, almost mandatory to be self-aware first. If that means to be self-absorbed, then fine. But that was only the first step. Then, you still need to be open and available to the other, if you are looking to fit in the 3rd layer of your needs in the Pyramid of Maslow, **LOVE** and **BELONGING**.

Now on this is would like to take a magical example that everyone knows. Look at a mother! Understand how a woman is moving up in status and in power as she becomes a mother. First, she took care of herself, feeding, sheltering, and reproducing. She found a mate and regroup in society to increase her chance of survival. Until that point, it was all about herself.

Then, something magical happened. She has to care for someone else as she gives birth. It will take her a few hours to readjust, but very quickly, she will regain the strength to support, and literally feed another being from her vital life force and her strength as she will be breastfeeding despite the exhaustion of the birth process.

And that was merely the beginning. Throughout her life, she will forever be bonded with that newborn she breaded into life that day, always putting the needs of her child before her own. But the only way to do that and to last was to ensure her own needs first. Of course, there will be some hard choices and a redefinition of her priorities but she will make it through.

What about the father? Most fathers will slowly join in that vibe too but Nature has made the woman in ways that her body and hormones are supporting that promotion. To the man, the cut is not as clear.

And when I said gaining in power, how many of you will stand between a woman and her child. You know that she won't be fleeing, it is going to be a fight to the death, moral and public opinion will be on her side. God will stand on her side for all that I am concerned. Would you pick a fight in such conditions?

I am painting extremes here to help you grasp the power a woman inherits as she becomes a mother. Well, she has become a force of nature, for as long as her child is concerned. She became that from her instincts and hormonal responses. Then, love follows.

She will give her life to protect her child, this is hardwired into her genes. But to increase her chances of success, her own self-preservation has been upgraded to new heights, not for herself but for her child. She must live so her child can live. And this is the way of life.

What I am telling you is to copy that template and to apply it to your own evolution. Leverage on your hormones using your emotions as triggers. Be aware of yourself first to gain the clarity and eventually the power to care about others.

Only by being self-aware can you find these true emotions of yours, those that define you at the core of your being. This emotions as you are letting them express themselves, those are the triggers that will stimulate your hormonal response.

"KNOW WHO YOU ARE FIRST TO BE AVAILABLE TO OTHERS."
Dr. BAK NGUYEN

On that, I would like to take a moment to salute all the mothers. No matter your age, no matter the colour of your skin, no matter your religion, you a literally making this world and the world of tomorrow with your embrace.

The world owes you a mountain of gratitude for the love, resilience, and passion you gave to your children and, by extension, to the world. When I hear about our society disrespecting women, it makes me sick to my bones. Ladies, without you, there is no world and no tomorrow.

Even with millennials of abuse and mistreatments, you found in your heart the strength to forgive and to keep loving. Your children grew from that love and, little by little, are making the world a better place in your honour.

In the name of humankind, ladies, please accept my apologies. In the name of the future, ladies, please accept my gratitude.

This is **THE CONFESSION OF A LAZY OVERACHIEVER**. Welcome to the Alphas.

> THE WORD LAZY IS WHAT PEOPLE IN CONTROL
> LIKE TO LABEL OUR YOUTH WITH,
> NOT JUST ON WHAT TO DO BUT ALSO ON HOW TO DO IT.
> PLAY IT SMART TO ACHIEVE AND CHILL.
>
> Dr. BAK NGUYEN

CHAPTER 6
HOW YOU IMPRESS YOUR CRUSH WITH YOUR LAZINESS?

"ACHIEVING WILL HAVE THEIR ATTENTION. OVERACHIEVING WILL MARK THEIR IMAGINATION."

BY DR. BAK NGUYEN

Here they come, the down-to-earth questions. Now that we have covered the definition of what is it to be lazy and to overachieve, now that we understand how to leverage our emotions into triggers and our hormones into kickstarts, let's put them into good use.

In the foreword, Jamie wrote something that surprised me. She wrote that this is not another book that will make you rich but one that will put your laziness into good use. Well, know that I am following the exact same path and that led me to Abundance, including wealth.

But let's apply the **POWER OF HORMONES** and of **ABUNDANCE** to this specific question to seduce your mate, in your words, your crush. This works even better since finding your mate is either within the 2nd level of the **Pyramid of Maslow** (to reproduce) or at the 3rd level (Love). The closer to the base are the needs you are addressing, the faster your hormones will kick in.

If I picture Jamie as a young female in her twenties looking for love and romance, like many of you, she is looking for someone to redefine her identity with. **LOVE** and **BELONGING** all merged into one big need. And where is sex in all of this? Well, fortunately for her, she will confuse the urge of sexual hormones to propel her desire, not to mate but to redefine herself.

This is where sex comes with a lot of strings attached! And that's fine, for as long as she knows it. By the way, I am addressing Jamie here but Jamie is simply the ambassador to all of your generations. On this, you can be a millennial or a baby-boomer or any generation in between, the path is pretty much the same.

So as Jamie feels her sexual hormones pushing her forward, she will feel hot and available to mate, to have sex. This is her sexual primitive instinct kicking in. But Jamie has been raised to have much self-control, so she will try to calm that urge and to let it pass. She still feels the urge and the hormones, and to hide, she will go to her head to find control and restraint.

> "DON'T STAND IN THE WAY OF A RIVER
> IF YOU ARE NOT READY TO CLEAN UP THE MESS."
> Dr. BAK NGUYEN

And this is what she will be doing, to block the expression of her sexual needs. The urge and hormones will be building up inside. It will become an obsession, now, not just to mate but also to control. Eventually, it will just explode and break down all of the restraints.

So why is it that Jamie and most of you, ladies, aren't just throwing yourself into the arms of the next random person you meet as your emotional dam breaks down? Because you have a system to contain that flood. You took your hormones from your guts and brought them way up into your head. That's how you kept control.

Now that the pressure is too great and that your emotional dams are failing, your hormones are rushing back down to your body. In the way stands another guardian, your heart. Your heart is much bigger than your brain. Your heart is also much more influential than your brain, whatever it contains will not take long before it turns your heart. And somehow you know that.

And this is where you become emotionally available to seek the love of your life. Is that young person your soulmate? It will surely feel like it since you are feeling all at once, all your repressed hormones escaping your head.

And *voilà, you are in love*! If the right person smiles at you at the right time, you are falling in love. You do not understand what is happening to you but suddenly you feel that you can fly. You feel free and secured all at once. And you will mate, body and soul. Your hormones have captured your heart.

And why does love not last forever, at least not the kind of love from the *Honeymoon phase*? Because your sexual hormones will drain out, until its next burst. In the female body, your sexual hormones are not as constantly present as in the male body, you will have those surges mostly around your ovulation periods.

So does that mean that by your next ovulation period, you will be falling in love all over again? Not really. The first time you let your dam break down, it contained the hormones and frustration of years of containment. Let's walk the timeline together, shall we?

You first felt the burst of sexual hormones wait back in your teens. Some of you will discover and have sex. From folklore, culture, education, and religion, most of you will not, before the dams break. How long will it take for the dam to break? I really believe that it will last as proportionally long as you've been trained and brainwashed by **Conformity**.

A few generations ago, and for centuries, Conformity said that marriage was when it was okay to let the dam down. When marriage happened at 13 or 15 years old (in medieval times), it wasn't that long. Then, with the evolution of society, we never cease to raise the age higher and higher. Today, in certain countries, at 18 years old, you are still a minor, a kid!

21 seems to be the higher norm accepted universally. Does that mean that at 21 you can mate? Not even in most cultures. You need to be wedded first. And then, only then, shall you let go of your sexual hormones… in the meantime, your body is still ovulating monthly.

With higher education and career, your life is barely beginning at 21. So most will delay for a little longer their *dam*. Doing so, they will have to build the *dam* higher and higher… until it all comes crashing down. And you will experience love for the first time. You will experience love for the first time, but sex, you will experience it over and over again.

You are not convinced? What happened when you are first falling in love, you can't resist touching him or her all the time. It is not about love but about touching and caressing all the time. The hormones are flying so high that everyone will notice. Your flower has just *bloomed* and its perfume is spreading in altitude and latitude. And eventually, it will run out. Once again, hormones…

Then, you do not feel the same anymore. That person who made your heart skip a beat, what just happened? He is not as tall nor as charming as you remember. And now, your couple's problems arise. Sure, you will try sex again. The orgasm will make you feel good for a moment but nothing close to the first few times.

Some will work it out and return in their head and heart to find the reason why that person they mate with is their soulmate. From folklore and culture, you are the princess who found your prince. You are finally living your *Cinderella story*.

The dress, the crown, and the chariot will be next. And you will draft your relationship to that moment of fairy tale you lived and relived a million times since you can remember playing and dreaming about the future.

This isn't the exact story of Jamie nor any of you specifically. It is though the blueprint that so many of you will walk and empower as if it was your own dream. Wake up, you are reliving a fairy tale written centuries ago and told and retold to make it your own.

Nowadays, are we any better? Sex is not as taboo anymore, at least for those with a more liberal culture and folklore. You will all experience the effect of the *dam* and the power of its release. And yes, it will be messy the first time. And then, you will face a choice.

Either you feel shame (because of culture and folklore) you will perceive the *mess* as a bad thing and will close down until you can hold your next burst. And that burst will happen, more violently and more frequently than you might expect.

The other choice you have was to let the gates open and to feed that hunger for sex as your hunger for food, daily. The choice is yours, is it? Sex isn't messy. It was amongst the primary needs hardwired into our core and code. If you do not have that gene, something is wrong with you. And yet, **Conformity** has us labeled what's natural as guilt and wrong.

If you still have any doubt about the lie and perversion by **Conformity** on our biology and needs, here is the absolute truth. In our modern societies, women may have sex in their teens but most will delay having kids after graduation after their career has kickstarted.

As their bodies were fertile in their teenage years and their early twenties, they have to either run from sex (abstinence) or run to sex with protections (pills and condoms). That worked for years and they had much fun. But is that enough? No is the answer to the majority of you.

Eventually, your own body will be telling you that it wants more and you will become obsessed with the idea of having a kid. Not all of you, but most of you. This is still a choice but the physiological needs built-in in your DNA and the release of hormones will be transmitting that message.

If no accident happened on the way, you will prepare for that event… often looking at the *white dress* and the *banquet* first. Oh, and what about finding the right mate?

If 21 was your ticket out of the gates, now 30 is your expiration date. As you are reading and exchanging, everyone, doctors and educated people you trust their judgment will all tell you to have your first child before 30. After 30, it might not be as easy… In our modern society, we call that the *biological clock*.

Between the career, the graduation, the search for mates, the debts, and the *white dress* and the *banquet*, somehow, many of you will arrive at the arrival before midnight of your 30th birthday. And then, it is time to procreate.

Well, just look for the statistics, the in-vitro fertilization market size was estimated at 14.2 billion in 2020 and is expected to grow 6.5% a year between 2021 to 2028. 14 billion to cover the natural needs for procreation. Are we in symbiosis with our body and biology? You see my point.

So back to how to impress your crush? I told you before to listen to yourself first. Look in the mirror, look at your History and try to understand what your body is telling you.

Is that a burst of hormones? Of course, it is. Now, if you feel that your identity will be better served giving in to that burst of hormones, no one can stop you. And trust me, your mate will see you coming. Just make sure that he or she is sharing the same interests and timeline.

If you look in the mirror and your own identity is cooling down most of your urges, well, you have just succeeded to build a new layer to your *dam*. Until the next burst, you are safe.

This may help you understand what you are experiencing and feeling but it does not help to seduce that mate or *crush* of yours. So what is the *lazy superpower way* to do so?

Well, leverage your hormones!

Your body is telling you that it craves sex and romance. Stop lying to yourself, to dim down the message and give into it. Empower it. You will change into a *beacon* attracting mates to you. Even if you had your eyes set on one particular individual, having the interests of the others will increase your chances of being noticed.

I am not saying to have sex with everyone coming to you. I am saying to free yourself and to be *available*. The bees are attracted by those flowers blooming, so you too, *bloom*. Having potential mates coming to you, the next thing you will feel is a boost in confidence, you are now the center of attention. Enjoy that ride, it just boosts your beauty by much.

And then, be direct. What I meant here is not to play mind games. As your *crush* is approaching, be genuine and available. Give him a chance to prove himself and give yourself a chance to embrace the day.

> "THE BLOOMING, JUST LIKE EVERYTHING ELSE
> IN THE NATURAL REALM DOES NOT LAST FOREVER."
> Dr. BAK NGUYEN

If until that point you lacked motivation, were trapped within your fears and folklore, leveraging your hormones will undo most of the harms and the false boundaries. But then, don't go running back to them as soon as the burst passes.

This was mainly custom fit to the ladies since I am talking to Jamie. How about you, men? Well, you are a little different, your biology is different. Contrary to the females, you do not have periods of hormones. Your sexual hormones are always present since the day you reached puberty.

In other words, you are always ready to have sex, to mate. What is stopping you to have sex all day, all the time, was how you perceive yourself.

For a man, his identity and esteem are directly linked to his sexual hormones. If we were all hardwired to *fight or flight* in extreme situations of danger, the sexual hormones of men will push them to find their fights, even to provoke them, as they are looking to feel who they really are: *testosterone*.

You don't have to be a beast to prove yourself. Nowadays, the ladies have broadened their interests in the male species. The Alpha muscular man is surely appealing to them but some will be attracted to intellectual individuals, some other to more moral individuals. The common thread is **Confidence**.

"WOMEN LOOK FOR CONFIDENCE."
Dr. BAK NGUYEN

Don't be over cocky, that won't help you. You can only leverage the attributes that you've received, so do not pretend, by pretending, you are lowering your chance of success to next to zero. No want like a wannabe, men and women.

Play your strengths with confidence and reach out. The ladies may be available but it is still for you to approach them and to prove your worth. If they are surrounded, it is because they are blooming. Cut through the noise and be the last man standing, genuine and true.

And how exactly will you do that? By overachieving whatever you were thinking of doing to seduce her. Do more, do often, and do again. Yes, doing so, you are showing your cards, not only to them but to your competition and to yourself. From your competition, only the strongest and most dedicated will keep on the race.

The real message was intended for you. As you are proving yourself, you will be doing and achieving things out of your *comfort zone*. You will be doing things you did not know you could do before. And you did all of that with so little.

You succeed in all of that because for a moment, you stop looking at your belly button. Your decisions and actions were aiming at someone else. In a word, you just **beat procrastination big time**.

Obviously, I wish that you will successfully seduce your *crush*. But even in the event of a failure, do you have any idea how much stronger and taller you just grew, especially if you had a rival as dedicated as you were to win the heart of your *crush*?

I wish I knew all of that when I was your age. But what do you want, life happens forward. Now you know. I will also say that I can't tell you with certainty how to seduce your mate. What I can tell you with certainty is how to leverage the situation and get out ahead.

You will succeed and you will fail. You will fall in love and be empowered. You will feel heartbroken and will have to grow out of that darkness too. Love and Life are messy and exciting. The only sure thing is that you will have to outgrow each and every one of these.

So be lazy and leverage your hormones. Be lazy and study the systems, in this case, *biology*. And one last thing, read the signs. Don't try to impress someone, especially a lady who is not available. You may win that one, but you are in against the odds, the winds, and the *dam*, hoping to still be standing the day she will be available. And that day too will come. Will you still be there standing and passionate?

This is **THE CONFESSION OF A LAZY OVERACHIEVER**. Welcome to the Alphas.

THE WORD LAZY IS WHAT PEOPLE IN CONTROL
LIKE TO LABEL OUR YOUTH WITH,
NOT JUST ON WHAT TO DO BUT ALSO ON HOW TO DO IT.
PLAY IT SMART TO ACHIEVE AND CHILL.

Dr. BAK NGUYEN

CHAPTER 7
HOW TO EMPOWER YOU TO TRUST YOUR GUT?

"DON'T CRAVE YOURSELF, FEED YOURSELF AS MUCH AS POSSIBLE."
BY DR. BAK NGUYEN

Now we are getting somewhere! You are asking about **trust** and **guts**, not thinking and secret anymore. Can you feel the shift in gears? This journey was about being lazy and achieving. This journey was about overachieving while chilling. Well, you just enter the vibe, the right one.

This journey is about feeling, trusting, and empowering; your emotions, your desires, and your guts. How to do so is to take the time to listen to your inner self without the noise and the filters. It is to empower your feelings and to use them as *triggers* to activate the biology (system) in you.

As you are responding to the stimuli (*triggers*), your hormones are now serving you to push forward. Until that point, you were wondering about motivation. With the emotions as *triggers* and your hormones as leverage, you do not have to worry about motivation anymore. In a word, you just **kill procrastination**! Think about it for a minute, you are feeling from inside your body the rush to respond, to do, to seek, to feed.

Then, you will need to face the consequences of your own actions and decisions. Even if the hormones won't last forever, facing the consequences of your own actions will keep you steady in action and in resolving mode.

Then, as you are not a victim anymore, as you have now gained the status of an active actor, *agent of change*, you are taking control over your life and journey. You are building

Confidence and with your victory, you will experience the surge of a new hormone, better than sex: the rise of **ENDORPHINS**.

That feeling is unique and better than most drugs. It won't cost you your life saving, just require you to do something exceptional based on your own standards to repeat the sensation, because yes, this is much deeper than a feeling, it is a sensation emerging from your guts and taking over your entire body for a little while. I told you, everyone who has experienced it will say that it is even more powerful than sex and orgasms!

And since nothing will last forever, the sensation will fade away too. It might fade away but its memory will haunt you. The only way for you to come back to that state of wellbeing is to come back with another win. And here arise the problem.

If you repeat what you did the first time, it will be easier and faster since now you have the confidence and knowledge to make it happen. You will experience the release of endorphins, but not at the same level. And the more you try, the less it will work.

You need to step up the notch every time, a little to push yourself against the wall and beyond your comfort zone to experience **endorphins** at a greater level. The closer you are to your comfort zone, the lesser the endorphins' release. So here is my *hack*: keep doing the same thing over again, faster and faster, I call that *aiming for your next win* as soon as possible.

Doing it faster will already solve partially your endorphins problem. Since you are doing faster and faster, even if you received a lesser dose, you will have your next dose faster than you think. What were your alternatives anyway?

As you are doing the same thing over and over again, it became easier and easier for you, so even if you are moving faster, it won't take much of your energy to keep the pace.

I don't know about you, but I am easily bored and I have a very short attention span. So to me, I can't keep doing the same thing over and over again for long before my own success turns into a burden and a prison. So to keep the fun in the game, I change the parameter just a little bit. Just enough to keep my interest and small enough to not affect my speed and its acceleration. This is how I grew from achieving to overachieving.

Trying something new, I kept my interest as I keep learning and growing. Doing the same thing (or almost,) I got better and better at it, so I developed expertise. And doing it faster and faster, I got my reward (**endorphins**) almost on a daily basis.

You were wondering how I developed superpowers? It was because I bathed daily with endorphins. I might have grown more resistant to its effect, just like any drug addiction will evolve into, so for a consequence, I pushed myself to score bigger and bigger wins. They seemed big when I stop and look at my achievements but as I am walking the journey, they simply seemed like the next logical step.

The more I grew addicted to endorphins, the more I need to deliver, bigger and faster. I told you about the simple law of physics before. Well, the laws of physic based on dynamic will state that the condition in inertia is not the condition in kinetic (movement).

The transformation for energy, from potential (inertia and mass) into kinetic and velocity will change the rules on gravity itself. Actually, the rules aren't changing, this is our perception standing in inertia and looking to understand Life and the Universe. The rules change because we changed state, from **inertia** to **kinetic**.

And the day my own mass (weight) contribute to my speed, that day, I became a tornado. That day I reached **momentum**.

> "A MOMENTUM IS REACHED THE DAY IT BECOMES EASIER TO MOVE FORWARD THAN TO STOP."
> Dr. BAK NGUYEN

Well, I told you that I am lazy, that you know. What do you think that I did reaching *momentum*? I speeded up, it was the way of least resistance. From achieving to experience endorphins, I speeded up to keep the hormones and the sensation alive, to experience a new way before the last one fades out.

To keep fun and boredom at bay, I expanded my horizons and tried new things, even if they were a degree of difference from what I knew. Doing so, I not only developed my speed and expertise of walking the journeys but I also became an expert in adapting, faster and faster.

Eventually, I cut most of the anchors down to move faster and freely in all directions as Life smiled at me. From a dentist, I grew into a CEO. From a CEO, I became an Industry disruptor and quickly rose into industries disruptor. Disruption was my constant, the variety of industries kept my boredom at bay.

From changing the world from a dental chair, I opened new perspectives and opportunities to the dental industry. Then, as I need to communicate my message, I discovered the book industry. Close to 4 years later, I brought a lot of new ideas, a library of books, and new ways, not only to consume books but also to produce books.

Keeping the same mindset, I am starting my new life as a *Dragon* in the financial and entrepreneurial world. It was not much of a stretch from writing books and giving conferences and interviews… until I found myself on the board of directors of companies aiming to revolutionize the world.

My keys were and still are, to be open, to adapt, and to repeat the process faster and faster. Speed helped me to remain lazy, as strange as it might sound. Openness brought in new opportunities and kept my interest engaged.

So do I believe in my guts anymore? Well, this is not even a question that I ask myself too often now. In the beginning, it was about finding motivation and the courage to go against the odds and the general opinion. Those were the **resistance** and the **inertia**.

In other words, it was a **dare**. Then, I had to believe and trust my guts. Then, I had to follow my guts and my heart and got into messy situations. My head got me out of the messes, every single time. I learnt and grew much.

Then, as I gain in speed, my velocity met with resistance. The fact that I moved quickly, I even won the race against resistance, doing and achieving before people could oppose me. As I stumble on that cheat, what you do think I did? I played that card, all-in!

I accelerated to reach momentum, moving from win to win, as small as they were. On the way, I got burnt and hurt too. Every time, the pain was worse if I stopped and looked at it.

So, I moved even faster to put a safe distance between myself and the pain.

This is how after receiving the Nomination of Ernst and Young for Entrepreneur of the Year, I went to new heights and fell hard from that as I missed the next round. Quickly, I replaced that shame with the scoring of world records.

Today, I hold status and record that no man or woman had ever reached, writing books. With 72 books written within 36 months and aiming for 100 books within 4 years, I am in a league of my own.

Resistance? Well, those betting against me, I barely remember their faces and name anymore. At some point, they could have joined me, they decided otherwise. Now, they hate me even more, not for what I did to them but for reminding them of what they are not and have missed on. To each our destiny and decision.

Resistance got replaced with *attraction*. As it became easier and easier for me to score and set new heights, I attract more and more people to the table. We share, we exchange, and with some, we decide to grow together. This is how the new opportunities came to the table.

Today, I am at peace with my head and my heart. I am also first and foremost, my guts. It is not about *daring* or *trust* anymore, those have no more bearing on me. It is about vision and fun, logic and speed. My **Confidence** took care of the other questions.

So to answer your question about empowering you to trust your guts, you have to experience the sensation first. Look for your next win and experience your hormonal system (responses). Enjoy your reward with the release of **Endorphins**. Then, you won't have as many questions to face anymore. And those remaining, seek actively their answers.

"FEED YOUR HUNGER. THEN GROW ENOUGH TO FEED EVEN THE HUNGER OF OTHERS. YOU JUST FOUND POWER."
Dr. BAK NGUYEN

This is **THE CONFESSION OF A LAZY OVERACHIEVER**. Welcome to the Alphas.

THE WORD LAZY IS WHAT PEOPLE IN CONTROL
LIKE TO LABEL OUR YOUTH WITH,
NOT JUST ON WHAT TO DO BUT ALSO ON HOW TO DO IT.
PLAY IT SMART TO ACHIEVE AND CHILL.

Dr. BAK NGUYEN

CHAPTER 8
BEING MOODY, IS IT GOOD OR BAD?

*"DON'T TRY TO CONTROL YOURSELF.
THAT'S YOUR CUE TO SLOW DOWN AND TO REGROUP."*

BY DR. BAK NGUYEN

Within this journey, you discovered something new, to use your emotions as *triggers* and to leverage on your Nature, utilizing your hormones to pace your actions and decisions. Hormones are *all-or-nothing responses*, literally.

Once a hormone is released in your body, your body will feel 100% of its effect until it fades out. You can still monopolize your brain to decide to act or not from the stimuli (*triggers*) but one thing for sure is that you will feel its effects.

That being said, if you empower your emotions and leverage on your hormones, what do you think will happen? You will feel stronger and frequent emotions, stronger and frequent sensations too (hormones). So in between the wave of emotions and of hormones, you are also feeling the craving of each. So yes, it is normal and most natural to be *moody*.

The difference is that you are not *moody*, victim of your hormones, craving, or desires anymore, you are moody because of the transitions from one wave to the next. This time, you are the one controlling the weather! How does that feel for a change?

You should be feeling great, free, powerful, and in control right now! And what does it means to be *moody*? Well, it's the sign that you are in-between stages, that your **endorphins** are running out or running low. Some will say that it is back to reality. Well, that's their take.

For those who experienced **endorphins** before, you do not want to go back. Now, hunger is deeper, now there are no desires, just needs. You can either put up with the craving or do what you already know, to come back stronger for another dose of endorphins. Do I sound like an addict? Of course, one addicted to success and overachieving.

I never want to stop or to slow down, not because I am a slave but because I refuse to die before I am actually dead. For as long as hormones are flowing into my veins, I want **endorphins** to be part of the cocktail. So when I am *moody*, that just means that I have to kick it up a notch.

The problem with being *moody* is that you give in to the emotions and lose control. I learnt a long time ago not to torture those closest to me, those I loved the most, with my emotions and lack of control. When I am moody, I take a deep breath and slow down for an instant, the time to regroup and redeploy.

For the last 3 years and a half, writing helped me to regroup and refocus at each chapter. *Moody*, I still am but not once, I gave in to any lack of control. I empower my emotions and let them out but only as I can harness their energy into *triggers*. Long ago, I learnt that bursts of emotions are powerful and can explode like a *hand grenade*.

I am holding the *grenade* in my hand but I have no desire to use that grenade to hold anyone hostage, including myself. I am not throwing the *grenade* away either. That energy is part of myself and throwing it away is a waste of my vital force. I am keeping my composure and dignity.

Yes, I am in contact and symbiosis with my primal instincts. I respect them and will not pretend to be above their expression. Thanks to that, I still have much influence and control over them. I empower their expression in a controlled environment and with the right mindset and preparation to harness their power without leaving a trail of collaterals behind.

We all know these people with much control over themselves until they snap and do horrors. Well, I am not one of them. I can't be because I do not repress nor accumulate my desires and needs into cravings nor frustrations. I just control when and where I can empower their expression.

And the more I let them out, the more they (my emotions and urges) have been kind to me. In one of my previous books, #15, **FORCES OF NATURE**, I compared my emotions to my power animals. Well, as I let them out, the first time was messy. I cleaned up after them. Then I keep let them out more and more often. Today, there is no more leash, gate, nor cage. As well-trained companions, they have become my ride.

Am I always in control? Well, no. But I am empowered and grown side by side with my emotions to learn to truth them.

Today, when I am feeling down and exhausted, my emotions are the ones picking me up. My *moody stages* have changed 180 degrees. To me, now it is a sign to relay the control for a little while.

As I feel *moody*, I can feel frustration, anger, lost, it doesn't matter. I can also feel joy, serenity, and harmony. One does not exclude the other, not anymore. Think of them as man's best friends coming to greed you. Play with each of them for a minute and quickly, the symbiosis will come back.

This is very hard to explain. I will address any of you who have the privilege of having a dog. Your dog has a mind of its own. It has a personality and will shape to fit yours. Well, as you grow to love your dog, you feel what it feels and will share. And this relationship goes both ways.

More than once, I came home exhausted and frustrated after a shitty long workday. Looking in the eye of my dog, HUSH, within minutes, she cleanses most of the bad feelings away, just by staring me in the eyes with attention and love.

HUSH died a few years ago but my experience with her has transcended into how I today, deal with my emotions. I look them in the eyes and we understand each other. Then, the cloud and the storm are gone, and I have my heart and mind cleared to move forward.

To me, that is what it is to be *moody* now, at 43. I isolate myself for a few hours, just enough to not do or say something that I will regret. To find a moment to take a deep breath and to look my emotions in the eyes, not as a dare but just like I once looked into HUSH's eyes.

In short, do not feel shame or bad about your bursts of emotion or mood swings. Acknowledge them and give yourself the time to cope and to regroup. Be careful to do that in private, to make sure there can't be any collaterals or regrets.

If you need some help, have yourself a dog and look into its eyes. It helped me to focus and to remain in control. Then, give back tenfold the love you received, to your dog, to your allies, to your emotions.

This is **THE CONFESSION OF A LAZY OVERACHIEVER**. Welcome to the Alphas.

> THE WORD LAZY IS WHAT PEOPLE IN CONTROL
> LIKE TO LABEL OUR YOUTH WITH,
> NOT JUST ON WHAT TO DO BUT ALSO ON HOW TO DO IT.
> PLAY IT SMART TO ACHIEVE AND CHILL.
>
> Dr. BAK NGUYEN

CONCLUSION
BY DR. BAK NGUYEN

It seems that we were just warming up and already we went through 8 chapters together. Coming into this project, I planned 7 chapters to match the **7-7-7** brand that Jamie is looking to launch as a podcast: 7 minutes of your day to change your life, 7 days for 7 weeks. Yes, stay tuned, a podcast, blog, and **UAX** album are on the table to kickstart the phenomena of **LAZY** as a series.

Well, she prepared 21 questions so I could kickstart the process of custom fitting my mindset to her generation, to your generation. I must say that it has been a pleasure to walk in the millennials' shoes and to share. By chapter 6, I knew that I couldn't finish this book with only 7 chapters, so I kept the dragon's number, 8, to fit this journey.

8 is the number of the dragon, in Chinese culture, it is the infinite. I gave you 8 chapters of being lazy to empower you and to open an infinite number of possibilities to each and every one of you. Trust me, now that you have the recipe using your **emotions** as *triggers* and leveraging your **hormones**, the game has changed!

That being said, don't be sad. Where one journey ends, another one begins. If from the beginning of this journey, I was addressing more the feminine crowd, because I was talking to Jamie, well, by the end of this book, you could feel the vision has broaden.

The next tome of the series **LAZY** will be title **THE ACHIEVE EVERYTHING BEING LAZY**. I will continue answering Jamie's questions but now keeping in mind that you have grown and are now ready for much, for better, for faster.

If Jamie said that this book was one to help you leverage your laziness, the second tome will be one helping you overachieve while chilling… being lazy. I can't wait to continue this journey with you.

From looking for your identity and seeking ways to motivate yourself, we discovered a *hack* to kill procrastination, a *hack* to leverage your natural system, and a way to free you from **Conformity**. I wish I knew in my twenties what, today, you know!

I must say how I envy you. I show you ways and *hacks* to save and generate energy. If you want more, I will refer you to my 53rd book, **THE ENERGY FORMULA,** a journey in which I literally share with you the secret of generating more and more power. This was a great introduction to the matter.

I envy you because more than energy, it is about time and its compounded effect. What you've learnt today will shift your mindset and results by a few degrees. On the other, your life haven't changed much. Wait to see how much you will grow and change within the next few months.

> "A BODY THAT REACHED A HIGHER LEVEL OF ENERGY WILL NEVER GO BACK TO ITS PREVIOUS LEVEL."
> ALBERT EINSTEIN

And so, even if you won't be applying 100% of the knowledge of this book, you have awoken and your life will change, for the better. Considering that you are in your twenties and that you will discover the **power of momentum** within the next few months, can you imagine how far and how much more you will achieve, discover and overachieve? Like I said, I envy you!

Remember that you alone hold the key to your journey, that you alone have the power to allow or not the influence of others on your choices, paces, and horizons. Much more than your parent and grandparents, your generation is very aware of choices and liberty.

Well, use your liberty for great use and face your choices, even if they get you in trouble, trust in your head to outgrow from the trouble you just got yourself into. There is so much more that we can do, each of us, before setting on someone else's turf and toes. If you go there, resistance and opposition will slow you down.

There are so many other dimensions and possibilities, if you listen to your heart and emotions, you will know. Stop looking at your head for direction.

> "CONFORMITY MADE SURE THAT WE ARE ALL AIMING FOR THE SAME THINGS, IN THE SAME DIRECTION, WITH THE SAME HANDICAPS."
> Dr. BAK NGUYEN

Before today, you were playing in a *poker game* having access to only half of the deck of cards, the lower half. By listening to yourself, by freeing yourself, by empowering your emotions and hormones, you are now playing, not only with all of the deck, but you are also holding the *dealer's odds*.

Give yourself a few months and read back these lines to know how accurate my predictions were. Until we meet again. Walk your journey and enjoy your ride!

This is **THE CONFESSION OF A LAZY OVERACHIEVER**. Welcome to the Alphas.

> THE WORD LAZY IS WHAT PEOPLE IN CONTROL LIKE TO LABEL OUR YOUTH WITH, NOT JUST ON WHAT TO DO BUT ALSO ON HOW TO DO IT. PLAY IT SMART TO ACHIEVE AND CHILL.
>
> Dr. BAK NGUYEN

ABOUT THE AUTHORS

From Canada, **Dr BAK NGUYEN**, Nominee Ernst and Young Entrepreneur of the year, Grand Homage Lys DIVERSITY, and LinkedIn & TownHall Achiever of the year. Dr Bak is a cosmetic dentist, CEO and founder of Mdex & Co. His company is revolutionizing the dental field. Speaker and motivator, he wrote 72 books over 36 months accumulating many world records (to be officialized).

- **ENTREPRENEURSHIP**
- **LEADERSHIP**
- **QUEST OF IDENTITY**
- **DENTISTRY AND MEDICINE**
- **PARENTING**
- **CHILDREN BOOKS**
- **PHILOSOPHY**

In 2003, he founded Mdex, a dental company upon which in 2018, he launched the most ambitious private endeavour to reform the dental industry, Canada wide. Philosopher, he has close to his heart the quest of happiness of the people surrounding him, patients and colleagues alike. In 2020, he launched an International collaborative initiative named **THE ALPHAS** to share knowledge and for Entrepreneurs and Doctors to thrive through the Greatest Pandemic and Economic depression of our time.

In 2016, he co-found with Tranie Vo, Emotive World Incorporated, a tech research company to use technology to empower happiness and sharing. U.A.X. the ultimate audio experience is the landmark project on which the team is advancing, utilizing the technics of the movie industry and the advancement in ARTIFICIAL INTELLIGENCE to save the book industry and to upgrade the continuing education space.

These projects have allowed Dr Nguyen to attract interests from the international and diplomatic community and he is now the center of a global discussion in the wellbeing and the future of the health profession. It is in that matter that he shares his thoughts and encourages the health community to share their own stories.

"It's not worth it go through it alone! Together, we stand, alone, we fall."

Motivational speaker and serial entrepreneur, philosopher and author, from his own words, Dr Nguyen describes himself as a dentist by circumstances, an entrepreneur by nature and a communicator by passion.

He also holds recognitions from the Canadian Parliament and the Canadian Senate.

www.DrBakNguyen.com

ULTIMATE AUDIO EXPERIENCE

A new way to learn and enjoy Audiobooks. Made to be entertaining while keeping the self-educational value of a book, UAX will appeal to both auditive and visual people. UAX is the blockbuster of the Audiobooks.

UAX will cover most of Dr Bak's books, and is now negotiating to bring more authors and more titles to the UAX concept. Now streaming on Spotify, Apple Music and available for download on all major music platforms. Give it a try today!

AMAZON - BARNES & NOBLE - APPLE BOOKS - KINDLE
SPOTIFY - APPLE MUSIC

COMBO
PAPERBACK/AUDIOBOOK
ACTIVATION

Please register your book to receive the link to your audiobook version. Register at:
https://baknguyen.com/the-confession-of-a-lazy-overachiever-registry

Your license of the audiobook allows you to share with up to 3 peoples the audiobook contained at this link. Book published by Dr. Bak publishing company. Audiobook produced by Emotive World Inc. Copyright 2020, All right reserved.

FROM THE SAME AUTHOR
Dr Bak Nguyen

www.DrBakNguyen.com

FACTEUR HUMAIN -035
LE LEADERSHIP DU SUCCÈS
par Dr. BAK NGUYEN & CHRISTIAN TRUDEAU

ehappyPedia -038
THE RISE OF THE UNICORN
BY Dr. BAK NGUYEN & Dr. JEAN DE SERRES

CHAMPION MINDSET -039
LEARNING TO WIN
BY Dr. BAK NGUYEN & CHRISTOPHE MULUMBA

THE RISE OF THE UNICORN 2 -076
eHappyPedia
BY Dr BAK NGUYEN & Dr JEAN DE SERRES

BRANDING DrBAK -044
BALANCING STRATEGY AND EMOTIONS
BY Dr. BAK NGUYEN

002 - **La Symphonie des Sens**
ENTREPREUNARIAT
par Dr. BAK NGUYEN

006 - **Industries Disruptors**
BY Dr .BAK NGUYEN

007 - **Changing the World from a dental chair**
BY Dr. BAK NGUYEN

008 - **The Power Behind the Alpha**
BY TRANIE VO & Dr. BAK NGUYEN

036 - **SELFMADE**
GRATITUDE AND HUMILITY
BY Dr. BAK NGUYEN

072 - **THE U.A.X. STORY**
THE ULTIMATE AUDIO EXPERIENCE
BY Dr. BAK NGUYEN

088 - **CRYPTOCONOMICS 101**
MY PERSONAL JOURNEY
FROM 50K TO 1 MILLION
BY Dr BAK NGUYEN

SYMPHONY OF SKILLS -001
BY Dr. BAK NGUYEN

CHILDREN'S BOOK
with William Bak

The Trilogy of Legends

THE LEGEND OF THE CHICKEN HEART -016
LA LÉGENDE DU COEUR DE POULET -017
BY Dr. BAK NGUYEN & WILLIAM BAK

THE LEGEND OF THE LION HEART -018
LA LÉGENDE DU COEUR DE LION -019
BY Dr. BAK NGUYEN & WILLIAM BAK

THE LEGEND OF THE DRAGON HEART -020
LA LÉGENDE DU COEUR DE DRAGON -021
BY Dr. BAK NGUYEN & WILLIAM BAK

WE ARE ALL DRAGONS -022
NOUS TOUS, DRAGONS -023
BY Dr. BAK NGUYEN & WILLIAM BAK

THE 9 SECRETS OF THE SMART CHICKEN -025
LES 9 SECRETS DU POULET INTELLIGENT -026
BY Dr. BAK NGUYEN & WILLIAM BAK

THE SECRET OF THE FAST CHICKEN -027
LE SECRETS DU POULET RAPIDE -028
BY Dr. BAK NGUYEN & WILLIAM BAK

THE LEGEND OF THE SUPER CHICKEN -029
LA LÉGENDE DU SUPER POULET -030
BY Dr. BAK NGUYEN & WILLIAM BAK

031- **THE STORY OF THE CHICKEN SHIT**
032- **L'HISTOIRE DU CACA DE POULET**
BY Dr. BAK NGUYEN & WILLIAM BAK

033- **WHY CHICKEN CAN'T DREAM?**
034- **POURQUOI LES POULETS NE RÊVENT PAS?**
BY Dr. BAK NGUYEN & WILLIAM BAK

057- **THE STORY OF THE CHICKEN NUGGET**
083- **HISTOIRE DE POULET: LA PÉPITE**
BY Dr. BAK NGUYEN & WILLIAM BAK

082- **CHICKEN FOREVER**
084- **POULET POUR TOUJOURS**
BY Dr BAK NGUYEN & WILLIAM BAK

THE SPIES AND ALIENS COLLECTION

077- **THE VACCINE**
079- **LE VACCIN**
077B- **LA VACUNA**
BY Dr BAK NGUYEN & WILLIAM BAK
TRANSLATION BY BRENDA GARCIA

DENTISTRY

PROFESSION HEALTH - TOME ONE -005
THE UNCONVENTIONAL
QUEST OF HAPPINESS
BY Dr. BAK NGUYEN, Dr. MIRJANA SINDOLIC,
Dr. ROBERT DURAND AND COLLABORATORS

HOW TO NOT FAIL AS A DENTIST -047
BY Dr. BAK NGUYEN

SUCCESS IS A CHOICE -060
BLUEPRINTS FOR HEALTH
PROFESSIONALS
BY Dr. BAK NGUYEN

RELEVANCY - TOME TWO -064
REINVENTING OURSELVES TO SURVIVE
BY Dr. BAK NGUYEN & Dr. PAUL OUELLETTE AND
COLLABORATORS

MIDAS TOUCH -065
POST-COVID DENTISTRY
BY Dr. BAK NGUYEN, Dr. JULIO REYNAFARJE AND
Dr. PAUL OUELLETTE

THE POWER OF DR -066
THE MODERN TITLE OF NOBILITY
BY Dr. BAK NGUYEN, Dr. PAVEL KRASTEV AND
COLLABORATORS

QUEST OF IDENTITY

004- **IDENTITY**
THE ANTHOLOGY OF QUESTS
BY Dr. BAK NGUYEN

011- **HYBRID**
THE MODERN QUEST OF IDENTITY
BY Dr. BAK NGUYEN

LIFESTYLE

045- **HORIZON, BUILDING UP THE VISION**
VOLUME ONE
BY Dr. BAK NGUYEN

048- **HORIZON, ON THE FOOTSTEPS OF TITANS**
VOLUME TWO
BY Dr. BAK NGUYEN

068- **HORIZON, DREAMING OF TRAVELING**
VOLUME THREE
BY Dr. BAK NGUYEN

MILLION DOLLAR MINDSET

MOMENTUM TRANSFER -009
BY Dr. BAK NGUYEN & Coach DINO MASSON

LEVERAGE -014
COMMUNICATION INTO SUCCESS
BY Dr. BAK NGUYEN AND COLLABORATORS

HOW TO WRITE A BOOK IN 30 DAYS -042
BY Dr. BAK NGUYEN

POWER -043
EMOTIONAL INTELLIGENCE
BY Dr. BAK NGUYEN

HOW TO WRITE A SUCCESSFUL BUSINESS PLAN -049
BY Dr BAK NGUYEN & ROUBA SAKR

MINDSET ARMORY -050
BY Dr. BAK NGUYEN

MASTERMIND, 7 WAYS INTO THE BIG LEAGUE -052
BY Dr. BAK NGUYEN & JONAS DIOP

PLAYBOOK INTRODUCTION -055
BY Dr. BAK NGUYEN

PLAYBOOK INTRODUCTION 2 -056
BY Dr. BAK NGUYEN

062- **RISING**
TO WIN MORE THAN YOU ARE AFRAID TO LOSE
BY Dr. BAK NGUYEN

067- **TORNADO**
FORCE OF CHANGE
BY Dr. BAK NGUYEN

071- **BOOTCAMP**
BOOKS TO REWRITE MINDSETS INTO WINNING STATES OF MIND
BY Dr. BAK NGUYEN

078- **POWERPLAY**
HOW TO BUILD THE PERFECT TEAM
BY Dr. BAK NGUYEN

PARENTING

024- **THE BOOK OF LEGENDS**
BY Dr. BAK NGUYEN & WILLIAM BAK

041- **THE BOOK OF LEGENDS 2**
BY Dr. BAK NGUYEN & WILLIAM BAK

086- **THE BOOK OF LEGENDS 3**
THE END OF THE INNOCENCE AGE
BY Dr. BAK NGUYEN & WILLIAM BAK

PERSONAL GROWTH

REBOOT -012
MIDLIFE CRISIS
BY Dr. BAK NGUYEN

HUMILITY FOR SUCCESS -051
BALANCING STRATEGY AND EMOTIONS
BY Dr. BAK NGUYEN

THE ENERGY FORMULA -053
BY Dr. BAK NGUYEN

AMONGST THE ALPHA -058
BY Dr. BAK NGUYEN & COACH JONAS DIOP

AMONGST THE ALPHA vol.2 -059
ON THE OTHER SIDE
BY Dr. BAK NGUYEN & COACH JONAS DIOP

THE 90 DAYS CHALLENGE -061
BY Dr. BAK NGUYEN

EMPOWERMENT -069
BY Dr BAK NGUYEN

THE MODERN WOMAN -070
TO HAVE IT HAVE WITH NO SACRIFICE
BY Dr. BAK NGUYEN & Dr. EMILY LETRAN

ALPHA LADDERS -075
CAPTAIN OF YOUR DESTINY
BY Dr BAK NGUYEN & JONAS DIOP

080- **1SELF**
REINVENT YOURSELF
FROM ANY CRISIS
BY Dr BAK NGUYEN

THE LAZY FRANCHISE

089- **THE CONFESSION OF
A LAZY OVERACHIEVER**
BY Dr BAK NGUYEN

090- **TO OVERACHIEVE
EVERYTHING BEING LAZY**
CHEAT YOUR WAY TO SUCCESS
BY Dr BAK NGUYEN

PHILOSOPHY

003- **LEADERSHIP** -003
PANDORA'S BOX
BY Dr. BAK NGUYEN

015- **FORCES OF NATURE**
FORGING THE CHARACTER
OF WINNERS
BY Dr BAK NGUYEN

040- **KRYPTO**
TO SAVE THE WORLD
BY Dr. BAK NGUYEN & ILYAS BAKOUCH

ALPHA LADDERS 2 -081
SHAPING LEADERS AND ACHIEVERS
BY Dr BAK NGUYEN & BRENDA GARCIA

MIRROR -085
BY Dr BAK NGUYEN

SOCIETY

LE RÊVE CANADIEN -013
D'IMMIGRANT À MILLIONNAIRE
par DR BAK NGUYEN

CHOC -054
LE JARDIN D'EDITH
par DR BAK NGUYEN

AFTERMATH -063
BUSINESS AFTER THE GREAT PAUSE
BY Dr BAK NGUYEN & Dr ERIC LACOSTE

TOUCHSTONE -073
LEVERAGING TODAY'S
PSYCHOLOGICAL SMOG
BY Dr BAK NGUYEN & Dr KEN SEROTA

COVIDCONOMICS -074
THE GENERATION AHEAD
BY Dr BAK NGUYEN

THE POWER OF YES

010 - **THE POWER OF YES**
VOLUME ONE: IMPACT
BY Dr BAK NGUYEN

037 - **THE POWER OF YES 2**
VOLUME TWO: SHAPELESS
BY Dr BAK NGUYEN

046 - **THE POWER OF YES 3**
VOLUME THREE: LIMITLESS
BY Dr BAK NGUYEN

087 - **THE POWER OF YES 4**
VOLUME FOUR: PURPOSE
BY Dr BAK NGUYEN

091 - **THE POWER OF YES 5**
VOLUME FIVE: ALPHA
BY Dr BAK NGUYEN

092 - **THE POWER OF YES 6**
VOLUME SIX: PERSPECTIVE
BY Dr BAK NGUYEN

www.DrBakNguyen.com

AMAZON - BARNES & NOBLE - APPLE BOOKS - KINDLE
SPOTIFY - APPLE MUSIC

DR.
Bak Nguyen

www.ingramcontent.com/pod-product-compliance
Lightning Source LLC
Chambersburg PA
CBHW071511150426
43191CB00009B/1492